My New Heart

Surgery by GOD

No Doctors, no drugs, no hospital!

GOD sent HIS Angels instead and carried away my heart disease!!!

Glory to GOD Series, Book One

Dusty Paxton

ISBN:1508845727
ISBN-13:9781508845720

DEDICATION

I dedicate this Book of Testimony to the only living GOD, without HIM there would be no testimony, or life!

My New Heart

    experience

        encounter

           and revelation of

     JESUS CHRIST, Healer

A true account and testimonial to my being healed of what the world says is the number one killer of women, heart disease. I believe what JESUS says, by HIS Stripes, I was healed....and I was and continue to walk, run, leap and live with the healthy heart JESUS gave me.

Enjoy and be healed in JESUS NAME

CONTENTS

Note from Dusty

As you read this amazing testimony of how JESUS healed my physical and spiritual heart, remember what HE has done for one HE will do for others, as HE is no respecter of persons! What do you need from GOD today? Falling in love with JESUS is the greatest blessing and gift I have ever received. Nothing is too hard for GOD and all things are possible to those who believe. I believe. I have encountered GOD's great love and gift to us all, HIS SON, and continuing growing in revelation of The GODHEAD: Father, Son and Holy Spirit. As you read the pages of this testimony I believe your eyes will be opened to an increase of HIS love and acceptance for each of us and how HE yearns for our heart to be one with HIS. My heart is now one with HIS, although for many years it was not. HE, in HIS everlasting mercy pulled me out of the pit and put me in the palace of HIS Goodness, HIS great love and kindness, HIS Grace and has restored true life to me. I'm one of those who needed an extreme makeover by GOD, and I received it, free of charge! The glory to GOD. There are so many testimonies I have to share with you and will but this particular testimony is worth a book all its own. Be encouraged, get right (if you're not through JESUS) and tight with GOD, you will be forever glad for it. HE is waiting for us! Don't delay, seek HIM more than ever before. Now is the time for your great turn around!!!

ACKNOWLEDGMENTS

I could not even attempt to write this testimony without the power, anointing and great leading of HOLY SPIRIT. I greatly appreciate the ministry of HOLY SPIRIT in my life, my very best friend.

Philemon 1:6

tells us "that the sharing of your faith may become effective by the acknowledgment of every good thing which is in you in CHRIST JESUS." I'm acknowledging that in the New Blood Covenant, in CHRIST JESUS, we received life abundantly through HIS provision on the Cross, HIS death and HIS resurrection, including, definitely not exclusive, healing. John 10:10 says "The thief does not come except to steal, and to kill, and to destroy, I, JESUS have come that they may have life and life abundant." Reconciled to GOD, sins forgiven, guilt washed away, no more fear, delivered from the bonds that tie us from being who GOD desires us to be, walking in freedom and fullness, joy everlasting and peace that surpasses all understanding, that and much more is life in CHRIST JESUS!!!

From Lost to Found

I think it's only right to share my testimony of how I lived before I asked JESUS in my heart to help you see how lost I was and didn't even know it. I hope you enjoy completely what you are embarking on and that you receive the revelation that JESUS CHRIST is the HEALER, DIVINE PHYSICIAN and HE wants to heal you everywhere, and I mean everywhere you hurt. Actually, HE wants to heal you in every area of your life that does not agree with HIS finished work of the Cross. HE died to give us life and life abundant!

Where to begin, I think I'll start at the beginning..."In the beginning was The WORD and The WORD was with GOD and The WORD was GOD" and as JESUS spoke, HOLY SPIRIT was hovering over to bring what JESUS was speaking into existence. The WORD became flesh and dwelt among us to redeem a fallen people and give life to us who believe on HIM, eternal life, true but also an abundant life while we are living here in this realm, time and season of life.

O.k., I will start a little later than the beginning of Genesis and the fall of man and the redemption of our souls through CHRIST JESUS, GOD's plan of salvation. However, it was in HIS plan of salvation that healed me of heart disease; the disease that the medical field states is the number one disease for killing women. I will start out telling you that I came (back) to CHRIST when I was 46 years old. At the first writing of this testimony it was 9 years after my return to CHRIST and I was, you guessed it, 55 and really glad to be alive. Today almost 9 years further in to this testimony I've celebrated my 63rd birthday!!! Yay, JESUS, staying alive!!! All glory to GOD!

I went to church as a young girl, received my first Bible when I was around 5 and a few years later attended catechism classes. I believe I went through the motions, hopefully meant it, of asking JESUS into

3

my heart at the end of the classes. Then at age 12, I was in church one Sunday and said to myself "if I don't feel any better after the service then when I came in, why do I come at all???!!!" That day I left church and didn't set foot back into church, except for a few weddings (2 of them my own) and another occasion or two for 34 years. Wow, that's a long time! Not that I wasn't asked by a family member or two, but by that time I was pretty much serving the devil, that sinful nature and didn't even know it. I never even realized, thought or knew I was lost and needed to return to JESUS and HIS ways. I never remember hearing GOD wanted to know me personally, that HE is my FATHER and really cares for me. I never heard or understood I could not know GOD, The FATHER, unless I asked GOD, The SON, JESUS CHRIST into my heart sincerely. HIS WORD says in John 14:6, "No one comes to The FATHER except through ME." I did not understand I was walking in darkness, even though I went to church in my early years. I had all the "good life"; beautiful, healthy children, a great husband, high paying job, a big home with all the extras, friends, ball parks, my children's school and sports to keep me occupied, alcohol and drugs for daily entertainment, family and friends at our home partying every weekend with swimming and games, nice, good-fun loving people, but desperately lost. I thought that was life and really good life. I was absolutely wrong. Even when my husband and I split (after 17 years of what I thought was a really good marriage, tells you what I knew), my Mom died, I lost a business I started, my living quarters changed considerably and my youngest child started going through rebellion and using alcohol and drugs. I still thought it was normal stuff, how life was. That is the lie I was living. I was deceived. But today, a new life in CHRIST JESUS for me, my daughters and their families. The glory to GOD.

Even as a little girl I prayed every night and continued praying every night as an adult. I just didn't know that I didn't know personally who I was praying to. Because I never understood that in order to know The FATHER, I must know HIS SON, 1st John 3:23. I never knew cursing or blessing for me and my family was my choice until I made the right choice and asked JESUS CHRIST to be Savoir and Lord of my life. I didn't make that choice without a few denials. GOD sent

4

laborers in my path, I just didn't listen to them. Right now I hear THE LORD saying, "there are some of you right now that are identifying with this testimony and need to come back to MY heart, MY arms are wide opened to receive you, no matter what you have or haven't done". If that is you, don't delay any longer, ask JESUS to come in your heart anew, now. MY sister told me when I was 25 I needed to come to church. My reply to her was, "when GOD is ready for me to come to church, HE will get me there". Now I know that was a rebellious, stupid statement to say! I was blinded, deceived, I was walking in darkness and had no clue that's what I was doing. Bang me over the head LORD. HE didn't. HE is a gentleman and would not force us to choose HIM. HE invites us and the heavens rejoice when we say yes, LORD JESUS, I need you as my Savoir and LORD of my life. Again, HE will not force us into a relationship. It is of our choosing. HE gave us free will to choose who we will serve; GOD or the devil. There is no other choice, if you think you are serving yourself, think again carefully.

There was a church across the street from one of the apartments my daughter and I lived in after the divorce. I thought several times, I should probably visit there one Sunday. I didn't. Now I understand HOLY SPIRIT was prompting me to go to church. A couple of years later we moved a few miles from that church. I had gone out with some of my siblings and their spouses one Saturday night to a local sports bar to watch football and drink some beers, share a few laughs with family and friends. One of those friends started talking to me about visiting her church, the same church I lived across the street from previously! I told her one day I would, see, still not making that commitment. Well, a few months later, after being out one Saturday night with family, same as above, HOLY SPIRIT (at that time I didn't understand it was GOD but that revelation came very quickly to me afterwards) woke me up early and took me to the church I wrote about above. My life hasn't been the same since. I liked it, I felt good going, and I started going to Sunday service. Within the next few weeks my other sister and her husband started coming to church with me. The enemy kept them out of church for a couple of years because my sister was hurt by the church she went to at the time. The enemy will do everything he can to destroy your relationship with GOD, the most important relationship in one's life. It was great, we were really enjoying going to church together and getting united/reunited with GOD and others. My sister's husband decided he wanted them to become a member of the church. In order to do that we had to participate in classes and Water Baptism, thank GOD for orchestrating all of that! That was May 1998. My sister's husband was diagnosed with a brain tumor and died four months later. I never thought much about eternal life until his death. It wasn't until experiencing how faithful GOD is, how HE prompted me to go to church and how HE made sure I knew HE used me as one of the vehicles to get my brother-in-law in church to witness GOD'S great plan of salvation. We knew when our family member passed that he passed into eternity with JESUS. Knowing and understanding more of GOD's compassion and love now I would have fought for his healing and deliverance. I just didn't know at the time what I've come to know about GOD's miraculous, healing power. Now, I would have sought GOD for how HE chose to heal him and deliver him from this cancer. HE is our Divine Physician.

This was just the beginning of my return to JESUS. The journey continues to be more than I could have hoped, dreamed of or imagined. The testimonies are countless of what I've witnessed GOD doing through a life dedicated to loving HIM. I have so many angelic encounters and visions to share with you and will do as GOD leads. I've even seen JESUS, more than once. HE is real and really wants to have relationship with HIS children. I'm more thankful today than ever that I finally said yes, JESUS, yes and look more forward every day to the awe inspiring life HE desires to give us. I'm so excited about the plans HE has for us who are passionately in love with GOD. Only because HE loved us so much HE gave HIS only SON to die so we could live....and abundantly! I have been delivered and healed from every evil work. My life has been restored to what GOD has for me and I can't wait to share all the times of turnaround in my life to encourage you to seek HIM for all HE wants to do in your life. I'm going to get in to the angelic visitation carrying heart disease from me now but I just want to say one little thought. He cares about every

6

detail of our lives. Just to prove that, a quick testimony. I was going to buy the same color eye shadow I used for years and an angel said to me, "go green", and I did. It was a little instruction but it was a makeover for my eyes. I can't tell you how many noticed the change. Small change with good impact for my appearance!!! HE knows the numbers of hair on our heads so why wouldn't HE know what color eye shadow I should wear! Right! Every detail, HE cares about every detail concerning us.

Matthew 10:8

And now, JESUS has given me the command, "freely I have received a new heart, freely I give".

On to my new heart!!!

JESUS Carries Away Heart Disease

A new heart without medical surgery. Can you imagine it? Walk through this testimony with me about how GOD healed my heart of heart disease and believe for any healing your body, soul or spirit might need and be healed now!!!

It is my desire that as you read this book and testimonies that GOD reveals HIMSELF to you in new ways, that you would have more revelation about what JESUS finished for you on the Cross and that healing in every area of your life is possible with GOD. GOD watches HIS WORD to perform it. HE is faithful and will do what HE says HE will do. Our portion is to believe what HE says through relationship with HIM, not just in the mind but in our hearts. When I came back to JESUS and started spending time in HIS WORD and prayer, in worship and fellowship with HIM and other believers I decided in my heart to believe what HIS WORD says about me. Not just parts of it, all of it. That HE loves me and by HIS Stripes I was healed. I really got a hold of what HE says HIS SON did for us through the finished work of The Cross. Not what my mind might say because until my mind is renewed and agrees with what GOD says about me, it is actually an enemy of GOD. Read in The WORD and get other books written on the benefits JESUS loaded us with as HE ascended back to HIS Throne. Keep pressing in and find that intimate relationship with GOD that HE so desires. Delight yourself in HIM and HE will give you the desires of your heart. Search for HIM with your whole heart. HE wants us to have more of HIM and we can have as much as we want by increasing in relationship with HIM and others. It is the only way to a life fulfilled.

Immediately when I came back to JESUS, I was hungry for HIS WORD. I spent a lot of time reading The New Testament, dispensation of grace, faith in JESUS CHRIST. Every time HOLY SPIRIT would highlight a particular scripture to me as I was reading The WORD, I would highlight the scripture in my Bible, write it down on an index card and meditate on it (ponder it, think about it, speak it out). For The WORD of GOD is living and powerful, and sharper than any two edged sword, piercing even to the division of soul and spirit and of joints and marrow and is a discerner of the thoughts and intents of the heart, Hebrew 4:12, study it. HIS WORD pierces the wrong thinking and replaces it with right thinking as you allow it to minister to your mind. Remember, we have to get stinking thinking out and HIS thoughts in. Renewing our mind is critical in knowing how HE thinks about us. GOD is love so let's receive more of HIS love and how HE thinks on us. One of those scriptures HOLY SPIRIT revealed in my early walk is "I will not die but live and declare the works of The LORD." This scripture has produced much harvest for my life, in every area of my life. HE tells us to seek HIM first and HIS Righteousness and all things will be added to us, all things, life abundantly. All the promises in HIM are Yes and Amen. Of course we have to be in HIM to receive all HE died to give us at Calvary.

I remember one Sunday Morning Worship Service about 3 1/2 years after I was baptized I had an open vision. In this vision I saw JESUS on the Cross; I saw myself go into HIM and then was lifted up and seated in HIM in heavenly places, scriptural, study Ephesians 2:6. A vision right out of The Bible, HIS Living WORD. This is one of several spiritual experiences that I've encountered revealing JESUS to me and who I am in CHRIST JESUS. I did nothing to deserve this revelation of glory. I will say the impact has been unfolding as these years have gone by. I knew it was an incredible, life changing encounter. I had the same encounter two Sundays consecutively. I was in awe of these encounters. I really thought everyone that has asked JESUS into their heart experienced this vision too. I was so excited and so happy to be in JESUS that I thought everyone shared in that joy. I was wrong. Many people wore long faces but claimed to know JESUS for years. I didn't get it. How could someone experience such

10

a life transformation and not celebrate the ONE it came from. Why were they there if they didn't want to celebrate HIS love. Had they really met HIM or were they just going through the motions of coming to church. Kind of reminded me of my younger days, why I left church to begin with. Now, I was alive, awakened and wanted everyone to enjoy GOD like I did. I realized that day, I was really touched by GOD, HIS SON and HIS SPIRIT and I believe it is because of the hunger HE put in me for HIS WORD and SPIRIT. Ask HIM to make you hungry for HIS WORD, HE will. Many of them at church seemed like they were in a dead relationship, they really needed a fresh encounter or the true first encounter. I know more about that today than I did then and won't get into it; but, if you are not having a real relationship with GOD, ask HIM for it. HE wants you to enjoy HIM. Keep seeking and you will find HIM. HE is worth the seeking! I just didn't know how one could have revelation of who JESUS is and not worship HIM with gladness, unless the heart got stony and needed some repentance. But, I'm sure that's not your condition. Anytime someone does not have a heart full of thanksgiving and worship for our FATHER GOD, SON and HOLY SPIRIT, they need to ask GOD to reveal what needs to change, how you may need to yield or repent, not letting "issues" get in the way of the relationship with GOD. HE knows the big picture. HE is bigger than we can possibly know and HE knows what HE needs to do in our life to be made in HIS Image. He wants us to recognize where HE is working in our life and join HIM in the work. One of our favorite things to do as believers is repent, turn from the old ways of life to HIS newness of life HE has for us. Of course, it's only through HIS grace that we change. When we seek HIM, HE pours out more and more of that life changing grace and our new life is revealed more and more. HIS plan is so beautiful for us. Receive a fresh encounter of HIS love right now. Let go of any unforgiveness you may be harboring. HE forgave us of everything we ever did and HE requires we forgive those who hurt and disappoint us. Ask for HIS gift of forgiveness and for HIM to help you forgive, HE will. Always remember, hurting people hurt people. Hurting people need the love of JESUS so the hearts can be healed and the hurting stopped. We need to see through the eyes of

JESUS. Look how HE forgave every sin of mankind, every sin, we are forgiven and we are required to forgive. HE even gave us that grace to be able to forgive. Then HE can heal the heart. That is for someone reading this book. It was not in my notes to write so whoever this word on forgiveness is for, forgive and run to JESUS. No matter what anyone has done to you, how painful and hurtful, JESUS knows and will heal you as soon as you give JESUS the unforgiveness. I have been deeply hurt and with HIS grace, I have been fully restored and healed. I may have to write that testimony one day. All of us will have disappointments and be hurt by people, sometimes even those closest to us, but GOD, in HIS great reconciliation, heals us and even removes the memory of it if we let HIM. I know. HE has done it for me, more than once. Wow, back to the new heart!

GOD was preparing me for things to come when I started getting that WORD, I will not die but live and declare the works of The LORD. But I had no idea what was to take place. GOD continues preparing me, as HE prepares HIS people, for things to come. Can't you look back and see how GOD has prepared you for things to come? I bet so.

A few other experiences need to be shared now for further revelation of how GOD prepared me for what was and is still (other promises) to come. A couple of dreams I had in that time period helped me to really get to understand GOD more and what the interpretation of some of the dreams and visions were that are prevalent to this testimony. One dream was I was preaching to a large crowd and I knew it was for another season in my life, a season after my new heart was received, but I did not know that at the time, I didn't even know then I needed healing for my heart. These dreams were before the doctor visits! HE always goes before us and makes the crooked places straight for us who believe. Then I had another vision upon waking up one morning. I was seeing HOLY SCRIPTURES being deposited into my spirit (the inner man), dropping from Heaven. I saw The Written WORD in book form enter in to my spirit (inner man), it was titled HOLY SCRIPTURES. HOLY SPIRIT revealed what that open vision meant, HIS WORD abiding in me. HE says in

HIS WORD, "if MY WORD abides in you, ask what you will and it will be done." John 15:7. With that I understood HIS WORD abides in me.

The following year HOLY SPIRIT kept me reading in John 3 for over 30 days. It is considered the new birth book in The Bible. We must be born again, born from above. All of a sudden this particular Tuesday night, lightening shot through the left hand corner of my bedroom. It was not storming out and there was no natural electric storm happening either. I believe it was demonstrated throughout the entire house where other members of my family were sleeping. I said "JESUS, I believe that is from YOU". I had peace and joy so I was reasonably sure the lightening was a good thing from The Throne of GOD, scriptural. I knew it was supernatural. It was an encounter with the Power of GOD. I just didn't know what all it meant. I love HIM and still today just want more of HIM. I have encountered HIM so much in this walk and continue growing in trust and HIS Goodness. Even for all the times I have messed up on my end, HE is the one keeping me and I thank HIM for that. It takes a load off! I continue spending time with HIM in HIS WORD and worship and praise is always a delight to me. I really have come to know HIM as Faithful, HIS WORD as true.

I remember any time the enemy would attack my body I would plead The BLOOD of JESUS over me for as long as it took for the attack to leave. Remember, by HIS Stripes, we were healed. There is power in HIS BLOOD; healing, deliverance and freedom in HIS BLOOD. HIS BLOOD was shed for us and it cries out for us continuously. To think the devil thought he won, if he had any idea of GOD's plan, he would have not let the religious sect kill The CHRIST; GOD's very plan of redemption, John 3:16. Did you know that JESUS took 39 stripes on HIS Back for the healing of every disease? HE chose to take all of our sins, disease and lack. It goes on and on what HE has done for us. Research proves there are 39 strings of disease, see, HE took one stripe for every string. Theologians say it was 40 stripes. I asked GOD, HE verified 39 stripes for me so I'm sticking with 39 stripes. I can't remember all the times that through pleading

HIS BLOOD, the sickness and other attacks from the devil had to flee and didn't rise up a second time. If any sickness tried to, I would continue to plead HIS BLOOD until I had the victory. I have so many testimonies that has happened in my life from calling on HIS NAME, pleading HIS BLOOD and The New Blood Covenant. There is Power in HIS BLOOD. What can wash away my sins? Nothing but The BLOOD of JESUS. What can make me whole again, nothing but The BLOOD of JESUS. It still continues for me and you today and tomorrow because HE is the same yesterday, today and tomorrow. HE says I was healed by HIS Stripes that were laid on HIS Back; HE took them for me to be healed of all disease. Who's report do I believe? JESUS' report in Isaiah 53!!!

One night I had a class at 7:00 p.m. Around 4:00 p.m. flu symptoms hit hard, really hard; fever, chills, aches, pains and fever. I was really weak but started battling, pleading The Blood of JESUS and praying in tongues, sometimes rather loudly and playing worship music on the way to class. I was not going to miss school. Even though it was in a close by town, I was going to go. I was not going to allow this attack to stop me from going and by the time I got to school, most of the symptoms were gone. By break, I was totally delivered from all flu like symptoms. Before JESUS, an attack like that would have put me in the bed for 3 days, but now, JESUS is LORD!

In August, 2003 I was fasting for 3 days. I didn't fast a whole lot then and still don't fast a whole lot now, maybe meals but not 3 days in a row very often. On this particular 3 day fast, I wouldn't eat during the day and then at 6:00 p.m. or after I would go get a Wendy's Frosty, it worked for me. Not too long after that fast I found out fasting from sun up until sun down was an acceptable fasting schedule in Jewish history. See, HE even kept me on an acceptable fast and I didn't even know it. I used to wonder about that Frosty (I could get too legal at times, all in a part of my maturing!) No more wondering. HE honored that fast just like it was. On day 2 of praying and fasting, having a great time in JESUS, right before I was on the way to Wendy's, I heard that still, quiet voice say, "I know the plans I have for you, plans to prosper you and give you a future and a hope." I was thinking wow, that's so cool, so awesome: it really stuck with me, a Rhema Word. At the end of the 3 days fasting, as I was turning my C.D. player off, I heard that still, quiet voice say "this affliction will not end in death." I was pretty excited because a man in our church was on his death bed and I thought GOD was going to miraculously heal him. That wasn't it, the man died. I didn't know what it was in reference to, until a later date and I had no idea the word was for me. That Rhema Word we need, we know GOD gave it for us and we hold on to it with true grit. Well, it was sent for purpose.

The next year, on a Tuesday morning in July, I heard a command "go to the doctor about your blood pressure." I knew it was an instruction from an angel, however, in my immaturity and knowing how GOD had healed me several other times by pleading HIS BLOOD, I questioned the source. For 3 days I questioned, GOD, did YOU send Your angels? I just didn't understand why I was being instructed to go to the doctor when GOD healed me other times. HE's GOD, HE purchased me through HIS BLOOD shed, as far as I was concerned I was no longer my own, I was HIS and glad of it. I had messed up enough in my life, but why was I having to go to a doctor. I thought it was a good question. I guess if I had thought it through, the enemy wouldn't have told me to go to the doctor, he'd rather I suffer, actually die is what he would have wanted. On Friday morning I was feeling pretty spent but I had committed to intercede for Pastors as they were hosting Christian television that day. I left after the show, stopped by the drug store and found out my blood pressure was over 200/?, don't even know or care to know what that number was. I went home and called a doctor that was close to my home and they took me immediately in for a visit. I had been saved 6, maybe 7 years by then, still a babe in CHRIST and had allowed a little concern to creep in, maybe some fear! I called my sister to tell her I was on the way to the doctor and she knew it was really serious for me to even consider going to the doctor. Again, because I had received so many healings already in CHRIST without the aid of the doctor! Only the Divine Physician. Well, against all I thought, believed, knew, thought I knew and believed, I left that appointment with a prescription and my sister! As I walked up to the exit counter to pay I looked up at the entrance counter and there she was, my sister, inquiring about me. I remember seeing this concerned look on her face. I had to laugh, smile and thank GOD that HE surrounded me with people in my life that genuinely loved me and cared for me. I was surprised to see her, she lived over 30 miles away. I think my first response was that prideful, "why are you here" but within seconds I realized how thankful I was she was there. GOD sends us what we need, when we need. We went to the drug store together to get the prescription and this blood pressure reading device the doctor told me I needed. I ended up taking a water pill to control the blood pressure. I took the pill and tracked my blood pressure readings regularly for the 3 months that followed. After that, every once in a while I'd go off the water pills because I still had this issue of "by HIS Stripes I was healed." I did notice every time I went off the pill I would gain 7 pounds or so even when I would change my diet. That was not good at a smidgen over 5', any extra pounds was not a plus by any means! Every 3 months I had to go get re-checked to get the prescription re-filled again. There was this particular time I went to get the prescription re-filled and the doctor told me he was going to put me on additional medication, I'll call it XX (not to protect the innocent, but to protect me). Then he started telling me, "once you start this medicine you cannot come off of it, this is slowing down your heart rate and you will be on this medication the rest of your life." I couldn't believe what I was hearing. I went home and said "GOD, this is not what I believe in, YOU'VE healed all my diseases, what's up?" It was one of those times I wasn't hearing HIM saying anything. I remember thinking, GOD sent me to the doctor in the first place, I guess I need to take the XX, also. Still I was bothered by taking medicine at all. I just didn't understand why I had to take medicine when HE has already healed me.

Now, I'm taking 2 medicines, as prescribed, taking seriously what the doctor said about the XX. That was a very serious instruction, I couldn't miss a day, couldn't ever come off of it. How did I get here? It got to the point the XX was holding me captive and I didn't even realize it; this had been going on for over a year. I remember being so diligent to make sure I had the prescription filled before I ran out or before I was even close to running out. It had control over my life. I had never in my life looked at medicine that way, it was really controlling. I can remember thinking, wow, how did this all happen. I'm looking to this medication to the point that if I forget to take it something horrible would happen. During this time I noticed my relationship with GOD was not as close. I would ask HIM why, no answer. When I mentioned it to others, they would say, "Oh, you're just in the wilderness, it will be great when HE brings you out of it." I had heard about the wilderness but really didn't understand that either. I thought well if that's it there is nothing I can do about it until HE brings me out of it. Even though there seemed a distance I still spent time in The WORD, reading and praying but it was like there was still something just wrong. I kept trying to draw closer but every time I knew there was something blocking the passage way. I know that by HIS work on the Cross, by HIS shed BLOOD, I could come before HIM freely. I kept praising, worshipping, reading HIS WORD and fellowshipping, but still I knew something had to change in the relationship. I also understood it was me that had to do the changing! I kept asking GOD to show me what was going on. I missed the relationship more than I thought was possible and wondered what I had done. HE would take me into HIS WORD and show me scriptures that I noted had the word idol(s) in them. I finally understood there was an idol in my life. I started seeking HIM to show me where these things called "idols" were in my life. I didn't even know if I knew what an idol was, I heard them described as "other gods" and I knew, or thought I knew, there were no other gods in my life.

It was several months later; I finally had a break through. I went to a doctor, actually a new doctor! I had moved and decided not to drive 30 miles plus to the doctor office every 3 months. When I moved I started thinking it might be time to find a new doctor closer to my new residence. On the way to work I would drive by this one office that got my attention and I thought maybe I will try this one out. Then came the day it was time to make the change. I shared with the women in the office I needed to change doctors and one of the girls I was working with pulled from the internet a list of offices. She gave me the list. The very first name on the list was the doctor's office I had been driving by on my way to work. The list wasn't in alphabetical order or anything. This doctor's office was the first listed with no rhyme or reason, it was wild. I knew that's where I was to go.

On my first visit the doctor shared with me how GOD had healed her of cancer and HOLY SPIRIT led me to pray for this woman. It was an awesome divine appointment. This doctor put her hands on my shoulders, ready to receive what GOD had for her. I understood she needed refreshing,. She had been working so much and just wasn't getting enough spiritual food. She hadn't gone to church in quite some time and needed a touch from GOD so she was soaking up HOLY SPIRIT. Truly, an awesome visit. I left her with such an awesome uplifting myself and the prescriptions necessary at the time.   Still on the meds, I had probably seen her 3 times. Each time my blood pressure reading was the exact same, it was really funny but I knew it was GOD. I knew GOD was up to something because sometimes the P.A. didn't even finish the reading. She would take the pressure band off and would always say the same reading, 132/80. Think I'm strange if you want but I know the angels were on assignment. It actually became very humorous to me and I would just smile as the P.A. gave the same reading. On the 3rd. visit I said Doc, don't you think it's strange, funny that the blood pressure reading for the past 3 visits have been the exact same numbers. She replies, "yes" after looking at the chart, end of that conversation. She never mentioned it again. As I was thinking, o.k. GOD, YOU are in charge! I still thought it was rather strange she never mentioned my blood pressure again! I was still seeking JESUS about what the idol was in my life. Have you figured it out yet? I had no clue at this point but it's going to be revealed to me soon. On the next visit, while sitting in the "waiting on the doctor room", you know that little room where the doctor eventually comes in and sees you? In that room, I heard HIS still quiet voice, saying the XX is the idol. Wow, my awaited answer! Really GOD, the XX is the idol??!! Thank YOU JESUS for revealing it to me. So, here comes the doctor in the room immediately after I heard HIM speak. I asked the doctor, "what do I need to do to get off the XX"? She answered, "we will get to that down the road, some other things need to be taken care

18

of first". She said it was a process but she could help me get off of them at a later date. Hmmmm, a later date, not the answer, better answer than the previous doctor had said but still not the answer I needed. GOD told me the idol that was a stumbling block in my relationship with HIM and I knew I had to act upon what HE revealed to me and quickly. You see, without realizing it I was looking at this medicine as keeping me alive. I was dependent on the medication, I was substituting it for JESUS' redemption power. Remember I had said earlier that I had to take the medicine and not come off of it for my entire life, that I made sure I had my refills in plenty of time? I would not miss a day in taking the XX because I was afraid of what would happen to me, remember those thoughts from earlier? I was really looking at the XX to keep me alive instead of GOD, I was depending more on the medication than GOD. The author of life!

I understood from reading HIS WORD that GOD says to get rid of your idols and return to HIM. Nothing is more important than my relationship with GOD so I knew I had to make a decision. I needed to repent and get rid of this idol. So, on the way home from the doctor visit, which was on Thursday, I repented. I knew I had to stop taking the XX, cold turkey as some say! I decided that day I would not take the XX anymore. I also decided I would not tell my sisters because of their concern for me, after they gave me their opinions, how they would be concerned and worry over the circumstance, all out of love. I was sharing with JESUS I understood that repentance comes with turning away from the sin and asked and thanked HIM for helping me come off of this medication. When I got up Friday morning, I went to work XX free, it was a glorious day. I was on top of the world, my relationship with GOD was better than ever. Obedience brings the blessing, my day at work was great. I felt great, free and even had some special treats throughout the day. I knew GOD was blessing me all day long!!! HE also knew what was ahead. I was just rejoicing in JESUS, having a great time with mine and GOD'S secret. Friday night, around midnight, fear crept in. Where fear is, faith is not! I started thinking about the "what if's", definitely not of GOD. I was listening to the wrong voices, those voices of fear. GOD would not have shown me the idol if HE thought I needed it to live, HE is a good GOD. I didn't think on that! I ran downstairs so fast, flew open the pantry door and got the XX, took it and went to bed. I let fear win that time. Wow, then it was like GOD, I'm so sorry and repented for allowing fear to determine my decision. I asked HIM for HIS help to make this right and get me right with HIM. The next night, Saturday, I was at fellowship and Pastor preached a message just for me. You know how GOD sends those messages for many in the hearing range, but at times we think it's just for us. Well, this message was directly from GOD to me. The message content was on substituting other things in place of HOLY SPIRIT and not trusting in JESUS for what HE accomplished for us on the Cross. Remember, I said HE healed me by HIS Stripes? That's me Pastor is talking to. After service I knew I had to lay the XX down, this time for good. This was in October 2005. After repenting again, saying "GOD, YOU are my healer. YOUR WORD says that in YOU, I move, live and have my being. I'm healed by YOUR Stripes. YOUR WORD says that if I repent and turn from my wicked ways, that YOU will hear from heaven and will forgive my sin and heal my land. YOU will heal my land and that the life I live in this body I live by faith in CHRIST JESUS, all scriptural. I trust YOU because I'm YOURS and I know I'm YOURS, I know I have been born again, born from above by YOUR WORD and YOUR SPIRIT (remember I shared earlier I saw HOLY SCRIPTURES come into my spirit and the lightning?), I believe by faith I'm YOURS. In John 6:56 it is written; "Everyone who eats MY Flesh and drinks MY Blood is in ME and I in him. I (JESUS) live by the power of the living FATHER who sent ME and in the same way those who partake of ME shall live because of ME". I partake of JESUS, I live in HIS power, not my own. HE purchased me through the finished work of the Cross. I belong to HIM. Amen! Powerful revelation. I hope you receive it in your heart as you read it.

Early in my walk as I was praising GOD one night, quiet time in my bedroom with praise music on, I heard in my heart, Psalm 91. I knew it was a Rhema Word for me to hold on to. I did and still do, HIS WORD hidden in my heart. Psalm 91 declares GOD will send HIS angels concerning us that are in HIS secret place (where we all need to be). Ask HIM if you are in HIS secret place, HE will surely tell you.

I've experienced angels ministering on my behalf many times and they continue to minister to me, with me and for me. That's a promise of GOD to us. Have you ever thought about those times you were prevented from being hurt, maybe in an accident that didn't happen but should have? Angels on assignment! Thank GOD, HE sends them on our behalf. I was so relieved after I stopped the medication, I had laid the idol down for good, never to pick it up again. Even though I was having symptoms in my body I decided I was going to trust JESUS, my healer. I did not believe HE would have me come off of the XX and then take me out. I believed in HIM, healing me. HE is a merciful GOD. Even when the symptoms were getting worse, I said no, I'm standing on the promises of GOD. HE will see me through this. HE gave me HIS WORD, before any of this affliction came on me several years ago, HE told me, "I would not die, but live and declare the works of GOD." Remember I shared with you earlier HE told me this affliction would not end in death? It didn't! We can always trust what HE tells us, always.

I was asking HIM what was going on with me? Why was I struggling so much in my body? HE took me to Exodus 15:9, "the enemy said I will pursue, I will overtake, I will divide the spoil; my desire shall be satisfied on them,"....Nevertheless, GOD said no and HE reigns over all things, not some, all. HE had already told me this affliction would not end in death as well as telling me my enemies would not rejoice over me. Hallelujah!!! I can't begin to thank GOD for bringing forth HIS WORD to produce 100 fold in my life. HE tells us, HIS WORD planted on good ground produces harvests of 30, 60 or 100 fold. Matthew 13:8. I reap 100 fold! Talk to GOD about the present condition of your ground, your inner man. Study Matthew 13, good ground produces great harvest. The more you spend time with HIM and HIS WORD, the more your heart rejoices!

I just kept going, many days not giving any thought to what my body was saying. I was working 40-50 hours weekly, continuing as though nothing was wrong, pressing on, in JESUS. I will admit there were times that I thought, wow, I'm not ready to leave earth yet, I have a lot left to do. A lot I want to do. GOD kept me in HIS Peace.

21

Sometimes, I would feel HIS wings of healing wrapped around me like so many of us do when we are spending time with HIM on a regular basis. If you are not spending time with HIM, you are missing out on the greatest part of this life on earth. Several times, only by HIS WORD, did I know I would wake up in the morning when I went to bed that night. If anyone actually understood what I was experiencing they would have insisted I go to the doctor and that is why I didn't share with anyone what I was going through. I was willing to find out what GOD would do. Occasionally, I would ask someone to pray for health for me without any detail but I had decided I was waiting on GOD. HE tells us to wait on HIM and we will be renewed in strength.

A determining factor. I felt led to go to the doctor at the beginning of March, probably mid-February but didn't make the call to get in until the first part of March. The Doc said she didn't like what she felt around my neck and sent me for a sonogram. I went, wasn't quite sure why I went. While the test was going on I was just thinking, what on earth am I doing here. After the test, I left, I did see some numbers I understood looked to be pretty serious but I was not going to take the medication to keep me alive. GOD either would heal me or HE wouldn't. I was trusting in HIS decision. I never called to hear the results, never answered any of the doctor's calls. I was not going to live by medication, that was not the life CHRIST died to give me or that I understood from spending time with HIM in HIS WORD. HE says HE is my healer. I knew I was in HIM from the vision HE gave me earlier in my walk and it really was to the point that I was going to trust what HE said and believe HE would bring HIS WORD to pass. HE did not disappoint me. HE never will. The WORD says man will disappoint me (you) but GOD never will. I believe what HE says. I had no idea what was going to happen next but I was pressing on by HIS grace.

The Apostle, Pastor where I fellowshipped, received instruction from JESUS to hold a conference the last week in April, 2006. He also received instruction concerning four women GOD wanted to commission for a particular Kingdom purpose. I did not know I was included as one of the women GOD was commissioning that night.

What a wonderful surprise. GOD loves to surprise us with wonderful suddenly's. What an awesome night. I was the third one to receive this assignment from JESUS through HIS messenger. This man, Apostle has been a true spiritual leader in my life, I knew he hears and releases what HOLY SPIRIT instructs. A man I respect and honor as flowing in the gifts of an apostle, prophet and teacher with integrity. He is also a man who GOD has used to bring revival all over Brazil and has ministered to countless numbers of pastors, individuals, couples wherever he is. A dedicated servant to GOD that I trust and honor. I knew when GOD speaks to me through this man that I can take the Word, prophecy and watch them come to pass in my life. In 2nd. Chronicles we are told "Believe in the LORD, your GOD and you shall have success, believe HIS prophets and everything will be all right!" I believe! I know JESUS talks to us directly today but HE is the same yesterday, today and forever and HE still speaks through HIS prophets. HE speaks to us, however HE chooses to; by the power of HOLY SPIRIT, HIS WORD, circumstances, dreams and visions and by others, even donkeys (if necessary) using the prophetic voice. We are a prophetic people. JESUS is the spirit of prophecy so we need to know HE speaks prophetically to us, HIS people. If we will let HIM and be attentive to HIS Voice, HE will put spiritual leaders in our life to increase our revelation of HIM. This spiritual leader I trust as a prophetic voice in my life. I believe in the Source the prophetic word is coming through when I know the leader is a true follower of our LORD JESUS. Maybe not every word we hear is from JESUS but the more you increase in JESUS the more you know what words are from HIM and what words are from the carnal nature. That is why JESUS tells us to test the spirits. When JESUS speaks it through HIS servant, HE, Jesus is the source we look to for the word to come to pass, not the man. Prophetic words from JESUS can save our life, keep us and bless us, protect us, direct us and so much more. Prophetic words are a portion of our inheritance for being HIS people. GOD loves to speak through us, to share HIS thoughts and heart for others. Don't be afraid of the prophetic voices GOD brings into your life, embrace them and ask GOD to confirm what HE is saying to you through them. Relationship with GOD is adventurous, definitely not boring!!!

Again, this is why it is so important to spend time in HIS WORD and in fellowship with The GODHEAD and others so we know how to hear HIS voice speaking to us.

After I received the powerful, commissioned packed assignment that night JESUS continued to speak to me through the Apostle, saying, "The LORD touches your heart, touches your heart right now, HE touches your heart. Let this be a sign unto you the heart of this woman is touched this moment in JESUS NAME. That which is closed will be opened, that which is constricted will be free flowing, says The LORD, every capillary of this body will receive the free oxygenation of this blood stream and her cardiovascular system is now refreshed and renewed as that of a young woman for she is a young woman", thus says The LORD. WOW, praise GOD. I believe!

I had never shared one word with the Apostle about my heart. He would have had no reason to release, decree and declare the Word of The LORD over me about my heart condition except that JESUS, who knows all things, spoke it through him. I'm forever thankful. I took this prophecy to heart. JESUS has all authority and power and I knew HE was the only one there that night who knew what I needed to live, abundantly. Understanding the prophetic somewhat, I knew I was on the way to total recovery from heart disease. I bind that word to my heart!!! How awesome is that?

I got up the next morning so excited and awaiting the fulfillment of the word. I already felt better just knowing JESUS was on the scene so to say. I was thanking HIM for my healing, new cardiovascular system, free oxygenation of the blood stream, no constricted areas, no closed or clogged arteries, wow, what a makeover, what an awesome Father. HE knows how to take care of HIS children. I have come to agree that FATHER knows best! Amen, Amen! I just kept claiming my healing from what I remembered Apostle saying the night before. It doesn't stop there. I knew I had some process to get through for the complete manifestation of the word to be fulfilled because I was still experiencing some symptoms but nowhere near what I had been experiencing. I was feeling good, really good. A touch from JESUS, the healer. I know at times when we receive our healing it can take time for the complete manifestation of the healing to take place in our body, life, marriage (whatever the circumstance). So we need to keep our eyes focused on what JESUS said, believe it until we see the complete manifestation, keep trusting and knowing what HE said HE will do, HE will do. HE is not a man that HE should lie, scripture. I believe GOD is strengthening us and developing our faith in these times of waiting, increasing our trust in HIS goodness. Will HE find faith on this earth when HE returns. That is HIS very own question. Our faith, trusting in HIM to be who HE said HE IS.

One of the members of our fellowship made C.D. copies of the conference and then went a step further and made us an individual C.D. for the four women who were commissioned that had our personal prophetic word on it. I'm still praising GOD for that blessing. You will understand more about that as you read on! I was really thankful for that C.D. because I couldn't remember clearly what was said on the commissioning and healing words and I wanted to listen and hear what GOD was saying.

That C.D. was a tremendous help. Anytime GOD gives us a word or some special communication, we are instructed by HIM in HIS WORD, to write the word down, write the dream, write the vision. So, with the C.D. I could do that and I did, but that's not all I did with the C.D. I would turn the C.D. on before bedtime, so low in volume that I couldn't really hear it with my physical ears so it wouldn't keep me up but my spiritual ears were certainly hearing it. The words concerning my commissioning and healing continuously played in my inner man, the heart was hearing and receiving the words continuously while I was sleeping. My spirit man never sleeps, even though the rest of me was resting beautifully! Every night for approximately three weeks I played this C.D., letting the words play throughout the night, letting them feed my spirit. Scripture tells us our spirit (inner man) is being renewed each day. Attending to the prophetic words are also scriptural. In 1st. Timothy 1:8, Paul instructs Timothy to follow after the prophecies made about him. The Bible is our instruction book and what Paul tells Timothy to do here, we being good stewards should do also. Right?

Right!

On May 18 while getting ready for bed I asked HOLY SPIRIT if there was any particular scripture that HE wanted to speak to me before I went to bed, any particular word for me to read before I turned the light off. I heard Isaiah 38:22, "Think of it! THE LORD healed me. Every day of my life from now on I will sing my songs of praise in the temple, accompanied by the orchestra", (The Living Bible version). I usually look up any word HOLY SPIRIT gives me in a couple of different versions so I can gain a greater understanding of the verse(s) HE is speaking to me. In the New King James version I was thrilled when I read the verse "And Hezekiah had said, what is the sign that I shall go up to the house of THE LORD?" Immediately I thought about the sign JESUS spoke through the prophetic word the Apostle spoke over me. Remember he said "let this be a sign unto you, the heart of this woman is touched...." Hezekiah asking about the sign, I never knew until that night the reverence Apostle spoke over me was in the book of Isaiah. What a wonderful GOD we have. I called my sister in the room and shared with her about the sign, she knew somewhat was going on but I still had not shared coming off the medication. She smiled big, said great and went back to bed. I was excited. GOD had taken me in scripture where a portion of that word was before I went to bed. Oh, I knew my healing was close. I just didn't know how close. I was thanking GOD, rejoicing in knowing my healing was closer, again, I just didn't know how close. I knew HE was the only One who could bring this healing to pass, HE did it over 2,000 years ago at Calvary. GOD tells us HIS WORD will not return to HIM void. It will do what HE sent it to accomplish. Those of you who think JESUS is not in the healing business today have been falsely led and are missing out on one of the greatest provisions of The Cross. Actually all of the provisions of The Cross are the greatest. It just depends on what benefits you are in need of at the time!

What an exciting way to go to bed. Psalm 103 tells us "HE heals all of our diseases," not some, all. Hear that, not some but all of our diseases. Remember HIS 39 stripes and 39 strings of disease?

At midnight, while I was sleeping, now May 19, 2006 (remember that date!) I had an angelic visitation. I experienced an energy flowing from the bottom of my feet to the top of my head. The Power, HOLY SPIRIT, Resurrection Life was traveling through my body. I heard an angel that was at the top of my head say "carried heart disease away. " I knew HE, through the use of HIS angels, (HE is GOD of the angel armies, scripture) carried heart disease away from me. At that same time I knew an angel was at the foot of my bed also, so two heavenly beings were with me to fulfill the word of healing JESUS sent to me. I was aware of them being there but I was so peaceful, it was like I was awake but not fully. Better than any drug could have ever done! Isn't that incredible, as Isaiah states it, HE carried our diseases, exactly what HE did that night, May 19, midnight, HE carried away heart disease from me. I knew I was healed by the Power of Almighty GOD through the New Blood Covenant in CHRIST JESUS. At the same time HIS Power was flowing though me it was also flowing through my sister who was asleep in her bedroom. It's for everyone in the house!!! Maybe a generational healing! HE sent HIS Living WORD and healed me, Psalm 107, of heart disease, really of all disease. No doctors for this heart surgery, only THE DIVINE PHYSICIAN! No surgery, no recovery time, no hospital, no medical bills. My own bed with peace, joy and a new heart, surgery by GOD. What an incredible healing miracle I walk in 24/7!

I asked you to remember the date, May 19! It has significance, great significance in my life. It was on May 19, 1998, that I was baptized in water for the forgiveness of sins and prophetically came up that new creation, baptized in The FATHER, SON and HOLY GHOST. Amen! GOD could have chosen any date, but HE in HIS greatness, chose the same day that I was baptized to send HIS WORD and heal me. I always look forward to every day with GOD and really look forward to those special dates HE just visits me in a special way and the 19th is definitely at the top of those days! I have other testimonies on the 19th day of any given month I hope to share with you at another time.

GOD is certainly into numbers, 8 is the number for new

beginnings, 8 years after I was baptized in water I was healed of heart disease. New beginnings!!!

I praise GOD from whom all blessings flow, what HE says HE does, HE does. We can always trust HIM to be faithful to HIS covenant HE has with HIS people, even when we are not faithful, HE is, scripture. By HIS Stripes, I was healed of heart disease, through the power of HOLY SPIRIT putting into action the finished work of The Cross. JESUS the same: yesterday, today and forever. You see, because of that vision of me going through the Cross and being seated in heavenly places I know the finished work of The Cross is mine. I have all the benefits of being born again, all that JESUS died for to give me. Ask GOD for dreams and visions to help you know who you really are in JESUS and what your inheritance is. HE will answer at the perfect timing.

I've been healed of heart disease and I believe this affliction will not rise up a second time, scripture. What JESUS does, HE does 100%, not 99%! HIS WORD tells us we are "overcomers." In CHRIST JESUS we have overcome the world, we are new creations. Notice that two letter word, IN. Having an Intimate relationship with GOD, being IN CHRIST and becoming one with our FATHER, JESUS CHRIST and HOLY SPIRIT should be the most important priority in the life of a believer. Seek, meaning to crave, pursue with all your heart to go after HIM first and HIS Righteousness and HE will add all things unto each of us. The relationship with GOD truly is the most precious, priceless and free gift available to each one of us. It is a beautiful, exciting adventure. Not always easy, sometimes even painful, but always beneficial to us who believe and know our GOD. Through HIS OWN BLOOD shed we have been reconciled to HIM, the one who created us and knows better what we need than we do. Our FATHER knows best.

HE gave us HIS WORD. We must be washed in HIS WORD, in CHRIST JESUS and baptized in HIS SPIRIT. We must be born again to walk in the abundance of life, with HIM. How do we get washed in HIS WORD? Study it, meditate on it, read it out load and pray for

HOLY SPIRIT to reveal the TRUTH of HIS WORD. Spending time with HIM in HIS WORD washes out the unbelief in our hearts, the fear in our hearts, the rebellion towards GOD in our hearts, the hidden wicked places in our hearts that we don't even know are there. Our mind is renewed by spending time with HIM, WORD and SPIRIT. Our minds must be renewed to the new creation HE has blessed us to be. Through the renewing of our mind we agree with what HE says about us as new creations in CHRIST. In the Hebrew, the word meditation is described as quietly repeating the scriptures in a soft droning sound while utterly abandoning outside distraction. That helps with the renewing of our mind. I believed JESUS healed me and wanted me healed through believing what I meditated and read in HIS WORD. Of course, we must ask HOLY SPIRIT to read the WORD with us so we don't end up in a legalistic mindset and miss the revelation of who GOD really is and what HE is desiring to accomplish in and through our life. We all have a plan from GOD that will fulfill our life, but if we don't seek HIM for it, we won't find it and we will be unfulfilled, our heart missing that heart connection it so desperately needs. Spending time with GOD, in prayer, praise, reading HIS WORD and taking time to listen to HIS HEART and see what's on HIS MIND is more fulfilling than anything else we could do, leading to greater intimacy. The more we know HIM, the more we love HIM and the more we love our self and others. The more we want to know HIM the more we want to be like HIM and we realize we can have all of HIM we desire. The more we can see HIM and the more we eat of HIS goodness the more we want to drown out the things of the world and be filled up with HIS purpose. I remove distractions, get in that quiet place and repeat HIS WORD, meeting with GOD every day, starting the day with HIM and ending the day with HIM not forgetting HIM throughout the day! I seek HIM and I find HIM. I have never been disappointed in HIM, HE doesn't disappoint, scripture. I am more full of joy and love than I could have ever even imagined I could be, all because HE gave me grace to know HIM intimately. My life has life now and has come into greater purpose and I actually see why I was born to begin with. HE gives me purpose and every good thing in CHRIST and I'm continuously amazed and awed by HIS Goodness. No one can out give GOD. HE created giving! HE has given me life and life abundantly. If you are not experiencing life abundant, don't quit, keep seeking HIM and HE will bring you into life greater than you could hope for. HE is our hope of Glory. CHRIST in me, the hope of glory.

I have so many testimonies I would love to share with you but in staying on point of my new heart being a testimony book all by itself, I won't. I just want to encourage you to truly seek GOD more than you ever have before. No matter how great of a relationship you have with GOD, it can always be more, JESUS made the way. HE is the GOD of more and HE yearns to find those of HIS that will desire the more HE has to give. I am so thankful to CHRIST for taking all my messed up life, and I mean messed up, the worst of sinners life and forgiving me for my sins (because of who HE is and nothing about what I did) and restoring life to me. What HE did for me HE will do for you. Come through The Cross and sit with JESUS. HE died so you could.

In HIS love and mine, wherever you are hurting today and need a miracle I send it your way: be healed, delivered, set free from lack and go forward and prosper in JESUS NAME, I release blessing to you. You say, I receive it. I pray that the testimony in these pages make you so hungry to have more of HIM and they encourage you to want more of HIM. My life truly has come from lost to found. I rest in HIM, I have my being in HIM and I live in HIM. It's the only way to live true life, and it is available to us all. So many people give up before they get there, before they get what they need from GOD, thinking GOD is not for them. That is a lie of the enemy because the enemy comes to kill, steal and destroy the destinies GOD has planned for HIS own. GOD is good and only does good. So, don't quit, don't give up, keep seeking HIM and HIS plan for you and you won't be disappointed. HE alone is GOD, there is no other and no other way to the abundant life without JESUS CHRIST at the head and in the center of our hearts.

HEALED EVERYWHERE WE HURT

JESUS tells us in Matthew 7:13,14 "Enter through the narrow gate. For wide is the gate and broad is the road that leads to destruction, and many enter through it. But small is the gate and narrow the road that leads to life and only a few find it." JESUS is the gate, the only way to life, ask HIM to allow you to be one of those "few" that finds and stays on the road that that leads to life. For HE will do it, keep asking until you know HE's answered. HE tells us in Matthew 7:7,8 "Ask and it will be given to you; seek and you will find, knock and the door will be opened." The devil has fooled many people into thinking that GOD doesn't want us to have the richest things in life. HE wants us holy and whole, HE died for us to live life abundantly. HE wants us to encounter true life full of bountiful prosperity and it all comes through relationship with HIM. Growing with and in HIM, it's all about knowing HIM and who we are in HIM. Ask JESUS to reveal HIMSELF to you. It's that revelation of HIM that converts our hearts to HIM and real life. HIS WORD says that if we delight ourselves in GOD, HE will delight HIMSELF in us and HE gives us richly all things to enjoy, a future and a hope. What an awesome GOD.

I mentioned earlier I have so many testimonies to share in every area of my life. JESUS is restoring me to who and what HE created me to be and HE is or wanting to do the same thing in your life. HE is the GOD of restoration and reconciliation. HE wants us all to live life to the fullest.

GOD has allowed me to speak, pray and release life changing miracles in people's lives. HE wants you to do these acts too. Because I have encountered and received so many miracles in my life, it burns in my heart to see others encounter these supernatural manifestations of GOD. These supernatural manifestation of living with miracles, signs and wonders should be natural to the believer. Remember, it really is part of having a growing relationship with JESUS. I've seen the captives set free supernaturally, the broken hearted healed supernaturally, I lay hands on the sick and they recover and raise the dead, spiritually and physically. These are all things that we do as true believers in JESUS but it takes being in relationship with HIM. Growing in HIS WORD and HIS SPIRIT increases us to have HIS Heart and release HIS Will.

I want to encourage you to believe and receive your miracle and expect GOD to move on your behalf. I want to remind us all how much HE loves us and cares more for us than we know. HE wants us to know HIS Goodness, and what HIS SON provides for us through the work of The Cross, HIS broken body and shed BLOOD, HIS Death and Resurrection and ascending to THE FATHER. We as believers encounter the revelation of all JESUS has done for us as we keep moving forward in HIM. We as born again believers are seated with HIM in heavenly places are dead to sin, alive in JESUS CHRIST. We as born again believers have been crucified in CHRIST, it is no longer we that live but HE that lives in us. We need to keep that revelation in our heart. Remember the finished work of The Cross, we are seated in HIM that are born again. We are new creations and were healed by HIS Stripes.. We must press in to find out who we are in HIM. We don't do that without relationship with HIM, reading HIS WORD and following HIM. We need to be in fellowship with HIM and others. Relationship with HIM and others are key to life abundantly.

If you are like me where you left JESUS and HIS Body at a younger age (or any age) and are just wandering without eternal purpose, please for your sake, return to JESUS and receive fresh life with purpose from GOD. I was the epitome of the prodigal son/daughter and when I returned to THE FATHER through JESUS CHRIST, HE welcomed me with all HIS love and opened arms. Just like HE will you. Read and ponder Luke 15:11-25, you will be blessed. I have a prayer for you to pray at the end of this writing. I'm still in awe of all HE does for me every moment of every day since my return. I have been radically changed and am so full of life. I don't want anyone to stay away from GOD because of things that happened in their life; no pain or anger is worth being away from GOD, HE heals the broken heart, let HIM do what only HE can do. The more we get to know HIM the more we know HIS good plan for our life. Believe me, it is a good plan but we must seek HIM for HIS plan for us to be fulfilled in HIS fullest of what HE desires for us. Greater than we could ever imagine.

GOD truly heals us everywhere we hurt. I have witnessed GOD and watch HIM heal my heart from past and current hurts, financial disaster, relationships, physically and mentally...healed and made whole by the finished work of The Cross. HE has HIS way to make us whole and as we continue to seek HIM for all HE has done for us, we receive so much more than we could ever hope for. HE is great and we need HIM to restore every area of our life. Living for HIM is the only way to live.

I know I have repeated some thoughts throughout this testimony but I'm so wanting you to catch all that GOD has for you. Don't settle for less. If you have settled for less, ask HIM to take your mess and make a great testimony of HIS Goodness through it. HE will. HE will make those rough places smooth, it's who HE is. Let this be your turn around time. Seek HIM and HIS Righteousness and all things will be added unto you. It just takes you surrendering your heart to let JESUS have HIS Way . HE is the way the truth and the life. No matter what the sinful nature or enemy sent your way, through JESUS you will be forgiven, forever changed and restored. What a transformation awaiting us. We are born again once, but saved many times throughout our life and walk with GOD.

In the following pages I have written prayers for you to pray for whatever you are going through today and to receive the touch from GOD you need. Agree with me in prayer and watch for the salvation of THE LORD to respond in your favor. Nothing is too hard for GOD and all things are possible with GOD. It's a win, win lifestyle. Enter in!!!

PRAYER TIME

My prayer for you, read it out loud and thank GOD at the end of the prayer for answering this petition!

FATHER,
I pray that every person that has read this testimony receives a special blessing from you, FATHER. I pray those reading this prayer are touched by YOU, LORD, and come in to a greater revelation of who YOU are to them and who they are in YOU. I pray that all needing a healing touch from YOU, JESUS, receives their healing touch now. I pray for the Spirit of Grace, HOLY SPIRIT, to bring restoration in every area of life for each one reading this testimony. I pray for their belief in YOU to increase and they experience and encounter your love in a greater measure. LORD, YOU have restored life to me in every area and freely I have received this restoration from YOU and freely I give to all those reading this testimony. RESTORE! I pray they receive YOUR revelation of the complete Redemption plan and as their healing manifests they remember to thank THE ONLY GOD who could heal them. For whatever they need at this time they will receive YOUR strategy to overcome and be more than a conqueror. I praise YOU, FATHER, for being a covenant keeping GOD and honoring the benefits in the NEW BLOOD COVENANT. I release YOUR healing fire into the lives of those reading this prayer, be healed in JESUS NAME, be made whole in JESUS NAME! FATHER, I thank you for answering my petition, in JESUS NAME, I give you the glory for all answers! Amen!

PRAYER FOR SALVATION, COMMIT OR RECOMMIT YOUR LIFE TO JESUS CHRIST

For those of you who would like to commit to or recommit to a relationship, reconciliation with GOD, through the only door, JESUS CHRIST pray this simple prayer out loud, believe in your heart and receive JESUS CHRIST as Savoir and LORD of your life. You will be forever blessed.

Pray out loud: GOD of heaven, I am a sinner needing a Savior, I, like everyone else, has fallen short of YOUR glory and YOUR Character and I confess to YOU that I am a sinner, needing to be washed from all sin, desiring to be reconciled to YOU, FATHER, SON AND HOLY SPIRIT. JESUS, I ask YOU into my heart, I ask YOU to wash me with YOUR BLOOD, cleanse me from all my sins and lead me in the path of righteousness, as YOU desire to do. YOUR WORD says to ask, call on YOUR NAME and believe in and on YOU and I shall be saved. I believe with my heart JESUS CHRIST is the only way I can be saved and reconciled to YOU, FATHER. Right now, I confess with my mouth and believe in my heart YOU, JESUS CHRIST are THE SON of GOD, who was sent to earth in the flesh, who's BLOOD was shed, to take away my sins. I, by faith, receive YOUR cleansing BLOOD. Thank YOU, FATHER, for your plan of salvation. For YOU so loved me that YOU gave YOUR only begotten SON to save me and I commit my life into YOUR HANDS through JESUS CHRIST. I believe I am saved now and not condemned. Thank YOU for allowing me to call on YOUR SON'S NAME and saving me. Salvation comes no other way than YOU, JESUS, and I ask today that not only YOU save me but YOU take the throne of my heart and become my LORD. I ask YOU, LORD, to baptize me in HOLY SPIRIT so I will have the power I need to live this life YOU have called me to. I ask YOU to create a great love for YOUR WORD in me, asking for revelation and truth to be sealed in my spirit, soul and body. Make me that new creation YOU desire of me and help me love YOU with all my heart, soul and strength. Help me learn to love others as YOU desire, LORD. IN JESUS NAME, I pray and receive what I've prayed for, the salvation of my soul. Thank YOU, JESUS!!!

35

Amen and amen!

Can you hear the rejoicing from heaven?!!! Rejoicing is exactly what is taking place right now. THE WORD tells us every time a sinner repents and calls on JESUS to save, the Angelic Host rejoice. They are singing in heaven for another one has joined the heir ship of CHRIST JESUS and has become a new member to the family of GOD. How exciting it is to welcome new comers in the family of GOD.

This is GOD's promise to you, if you accept JESUS, GOD will accept you. As you prayed that prayer, you accepted JESUS as your Savoir and FATHER GOD accepts you as HIS child. Romans 10:13 says "For whosoever shall call upon the NAME of THE LORD, shall be saved." You called on HIM, THE SAVIOR and now depend and trust in HIM to save you. Believe it, even when the enemy tries to say to your mind, you're not saved. Remember GOD is not a liar, HE is all TRUTH, it's the devil that is the father of lies. Call on JESUS' NAME and the devil will flee from your thoughts. As you call on JESUS to save you've started on your born again adventure, the greatest adventure we can ever take! THE WORD tells us we didn't call on HIM, HE chose us and we heard HIM and asked HIM in our heart. HE's a good GOD, and really only does good. You will find that out the more time you spend with HIM! The Gospel of JESUS CHRIST is true! Start asking GOD where HE would have you fellowship with your new family, the family of GOD. Start reading the Gospel of John and then the other gospels until you have more revelation of HIM and you know that you've had your heart conversion so you will know who you are in your new identity in JESUS. I promise there is nothing better than this relationship, nothing. Everything pertaining to life come from the source of life, JESUS. Just ask JESUS to help you have an intimate relationship with HIM. As you spend time with HIM by reading HIS WORD, praying, singing to HIM and fellowshipping with true believers you will be forever grateful HE saved you and you get to encounter HIM daily. Nothing in life can replace or take the place of a relationship with GOD in CHRIST JESUS. Welcome in JESUS NAME to our family. Now go celebrate being born-again and enjoy JESUS!

In prayer, just have conversation with GOD Matthew 6 has a prayer than covers your overall needs and is a great place to start in prayer but remember it's not about building a doctrine, it's about building a relationship. I remember when I was first saved I would cry out and say "JESUS, I don't even know how to love YOU or pray to YOU or praise YOU" and HE heard my cry and has never let me down. HE knows where we are at and what we need to have that bountiful relationship with HIM and HE wants it as much as we need it! HE is for us!!!

I bless you and yours in the name above all names,   JESUS CHRIST and pray for your relationship with GOD to grow in love and grace. Remember, HE is love.

In HIS love,
Dusty

Until we meet again!

As I have written I have so many more testimonies to share with you. Testimonies concerning: finances, (who couldn't use some encouragement on getting to know GOD as PROVIDER), so many more on The DIVINE PHYSICIAN, how HE delivered me from addictive behavior(s) (most everyone needs that revelation), HE is THE DELIVERER, HE is the Great GOD of reconciliation (any relationships need healing in your life?), experiencing and encountering GOD dreams and visions, the list goes on and on for years! I write these testimonies to glorify GOD and to encourage and edify you to trust in GOD for your life of abundance while here on earth. You see, we are to bring HIS Kingdom on this earth and testimonies is one of the greatest ways to reveal this Great, and I do mean Great GOD to all of the world. It is my desire that you would so expect GOD to reveal HIS Goodness to you and trust HIM for bigger and greater things in your life so you can be sharing more testimonies with those GOD puts in your path. To see GOD fully restore my life, making it better than I could imagine gives me great understanding that HE wants to fully restore every life that is willing to come to HIM and trust HIM as the GOD we so desperately need as GOD in our life. Because HE lives we can face tomorrow with peace, joy, love, kindness, faithfulness, patience, goodness, gentleness and self control. Let's do it! Choose to live GOD'S way and show the world how great HE is. He is our answer to all we need and desire. I look forward to spending time with you again through my other books or even in a meeting. If you would like to contact me please email me at newheartministries@gmail.com!

ABOUT THE AUTHOR

Visionary and founder of New Heart Ministries, ordained by GOD and confirmed by man as a 5 fold ministry gift to the Body of CHRIST. Emissary of JESUS CHRIST, Senior Pastor and leader of City on a Hill United Worship Center. Author, Preacher and Teacher who carries an anointing for healing, miracles, signs and wonders and who enjoys helping people become who GOD created them to be, but most importantly is her love relationship with GOD and man. She has been sent by JESUS to set the captives free, heal the brokenhearted, bring beauty for ashes, lay hands on the sick and they recover, open blind eyes and edify, equip and train the body of CHRIST, the army of GOD. Dusty also is used by GOD mightily to restore, reform and transform individual lives and ministries. Anointed and appointed by GOD to be circulated into HIS Body, bringing refreshing everywhere she goes!

CONTACT INFORMATION

EMAIL:
NEWHEARTMINISTRIES@GMAIL.COM

BASE LOCATION OF MINISTRY
JACKSONVILLE, FL.

GIVING GOD ALL THE GLORY AND FIRSTFRUITS FOR HIS GOODNESS.

PROCEEDS FROM THIS TESTIMONY WILL GO INTO MISSIONS. FOR GOD'S MESSENGERS TO TAKE THE MESSAGE INTO THE NATIONS, JESUS IS LORD!!!

Made in the USA
Columbia, SC
18 March 2021

34652565R00028